★ IT'S MY STATE! ★

Alabama

Joyce Hart

 Marshall Cavendish
Benchmark

Marshall Cavendish Benchmark
99 White Plains Road
Tarrytown, New York 10591-9001
www.marshallcavendish.us

Library of Congress Cataloging-in-Publication Data

Hart, Joyce, 1954-
Alabama / by Joyce Hart.
p. cm. -- (It's my state!)
Summary: "Surveys the history, geography, economy, and people of
Alabama"--Provided by publisher.
Includes bibliographical references and index.
ISBN 0-7614-1925-X
1. Alabama--Juvenile literature. I. Title. II. Series.

F326.3.H37 2006
976.1--dc22

2005017958

Photo research by Candlepants Incorporated

Cover photograph: Jane Sapinsky / SuperStock

Back cover illustration: The license plate shows Alabama's postal abbreviation followed by its year of statehood.

The photographs in this book are used by permission and through the courtesy of: *Corbis:* 20, 35, 36, 43 (bottom); Bettmann, 38, 43 (top), 50 (top); Raymond Gehman, 8, 9, 46; Annie Griffiths Belt, 13; Kevin Fleming, 16; Buddy Mays, 17, 44; Richard A. Cooke, 22; Flip Schulke, 39, 55; Warren Faidley, 41; Richard T. Nowitz, 42; Charles Rotkin, 48; John Springer Collection, 50 (middle); NASA/Roger Ressmeyer, 50 (bottom); Reuters, 51 (top); Hulton-Deutsch Collection, 51 (bottom); Lowell Georgia, 64; William A. Bake, 66; Bill Varie, 69; Greg Smith, 70; Spencer Jones/PictureArts, 72 (bottom); Philip Gould, 73 (top); Roger Ressmeyer, 73 (middle). *SuperStock:* 37; Richard Cummins, 10, 62; Prisma, 11, 58; age fotostock, 15; David David Gallery, 27. *Photo Researchers, Inc.:* David Hosking, 4 (middle); Joseph T. & Suzanne L. Collins, 5 (top); Gilbert S. Grant, 5 (middle); Doug Martin, 5 (bottom); Millard H. Sharp, 18 (top); Stephen J. Krasemann, 18 (bottom), 19 (top); Susan Leavines Harris, 19 (middle); Michael P. Gadomski, 19 (bottom); John W. Bova, 56; U.S. Department of Agriculture, 68; Dan Guravich, 72 (top); M.E. Warren, 72 (middle). *Animals Animals:* Maresa Pryor, 4 (top); Joyce Wilson, 4 (bottom); David M. Dennis, 18 (middle). *Northwind Pictures:* 25, 29, 32, 33. *The Image Works:* Jeff Greenberg, 49, 54, 57. *Associated Press:* Robert Sutton, 51 (bottom). *Mark Gibson Stock Photography:* 53.

Book design by Anahid Hamparian

Printed in Malaysia

1 3 5 6 4 2

Contents

A Quick Look at Alabama

Nickname: Heart of Dixie or Yellowhammer State
Population: 4,557,808 (2005 estimate)
Statehood: December 14, 1819

Tree: Longleaf Pine

Officially named as the state tree in 1997, the southern longleaf pine grows in forests throughout the southern portions of Alabama. This pine tree has twelve-inch-long needles that grow in clusters of three.

Bird: Yellowhammer

One of the unofficial nicknames of Alabama comes from this small bird. The yellowhammer is also called a flicker and is a member of the woodpecker family. The male yellowhammers have yellow feathers in their wings, but both males and females have sharp claws to help them cling to the sides of the tree trunks.

Wildflower: Camellia

In 1959, the state government changed the official state flower from the goldenrod—which many people thought of as a weed because it is a wild flower—to the pretty, bright pink camellia. The state legislature confirmed this in 1999. The camellia is a medium-sized flower that has several overlapping petals and looks a little bit like a rose.

Reptile: Alabama Red-Bellied Turtle

The Alabama red-bellied turtle is native to Alabama and lives in either fresh or brackish (somewhat salty) water in the Mobile Delta and in the waters of Baldwin County. One of the most interesting things about this turtle is that in the wild it only lives in Alabama. The Alabama red-bellied turtle was placed on the U. S. Fish and Wildlife Service's Endangered Species List in 1987.

Nut: Pecan

Pecan trees thrive in Alabama, so it comes as no surprise that the pecan was named the state nut in 1982. The pecan nut grows inside a thin, oval shell that is easy to crack. The sweet nut is a popular snack and is used in many southern recipes.

Rock: Marble

Alabama is known around the world for its marble, a rock that is made up of the re-crystallized minerals limestone or dolomite. Marble comes in a variety of colors such as pink, red, gray, and black. Most of Alabama's marble is found in Talladega County from the Coosa River southward. In the past, Alabama's marble was used in making monuments and buildings. Today it is also ground up and used in such products as soil conditioners, paints, and plastics. Marble was made the state rock in 1969.

ALABAMA

Florence
Tennessee River
U.S Rocket Center & Space Camp
Huntsville

Anniston

Birmingham

N
W   E
S

Tuscaloosa

Sipsey River
Coosa River

Demopolis
Selma
Montgomery
Auburn
Eufaula

Chattahoochee River

Jackson
Alabama River
Tombigbee River

Conecuh River
Pea River
Enterprise
Dothan

Mobile River
Tensaw River
Mobile

Mississippi Sound

GULF OF MEXICO

1 **Heart of Dixie**

Alabama is located in the southeastern part of the United States. Its geography varies from forested mountains in the north to sandy beaches along the Gulf of Mexico in the south. With its gentle climate and friendly people, Alabama is a great place to live.

Alabama covers more than 52,000 square miles, making it the thirtieth-largest state. Alabama is almost rectangular in shape, measuring about 300 miles north to south and about 200 miles east to west. The land surface of the southern portion of the state is made up of low hills and flat valleys. But as you travel from Mobile in the southwest to the Appalachian Mountains in the northeast, the elevation of the land slowly rises, changing from sea level to almost 2,000 feet. If you completed a tour of the entire state, you would see everything from sandy shorelines, to fertile

Alabama's Borders
North: Tennessee
South: Florida and the Gulf of Mexico
East: Georgia
West: Mississippi

valleys, broad prairies, swampy bogs, limestone caves, evergreen forests, and rocky mountainsides. Scientists have studied these features and have divided Alabama into six different regions, each with its own distinctive traits.

The East Gulf Coastal Plain

The largest region is the East Gulf Coastal Plain, which covers most of the southern and western parts of Alabama. In the southern part of this plain is the Mobile River Delta, where swamplands drain into the Gulf of Mexico. Also found here is Alabama's major seaport.

In the northern part of the plain, which stretches almost to Tennessee, the land is creased with rows of hills that run in an east-to-west pattern. You will find farmlands and forests in this area. Farther east on the plain, cows, pigs, and poultry are raised. Peanut crops are also grown in the region. Large

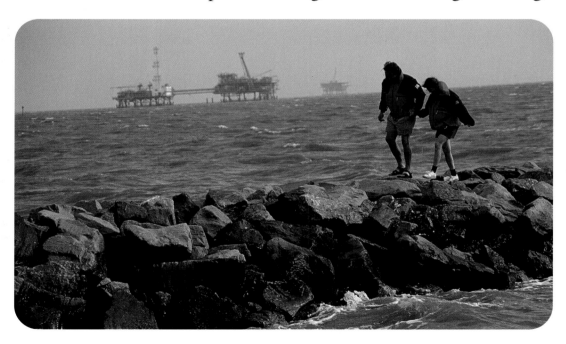

Beachgoers walk along part of Mobile Bay's rocky shoreline.

cities in this area include Mobile in the far south, Montgomery in the central portion, and Tuscaloosa, farther north.

Right in the middle of the East Gulf Coastal Plain is the Black Belt, which runs along the Alabama River Valley. This strip of prairie land almost cuts the state in two, dividing northern and southern Alabama. This region got its name because of its black, sticky soil, which was, at one time, a great place to grow cotton. Today, farmers who live in this area mostly raise livestock. Selma is the major city here.

The Piedmont Plateau

Northeast of the Black Belt region is the Piedmont Plateau. The highest point in Alabama, Mount Cheaha, which stretches

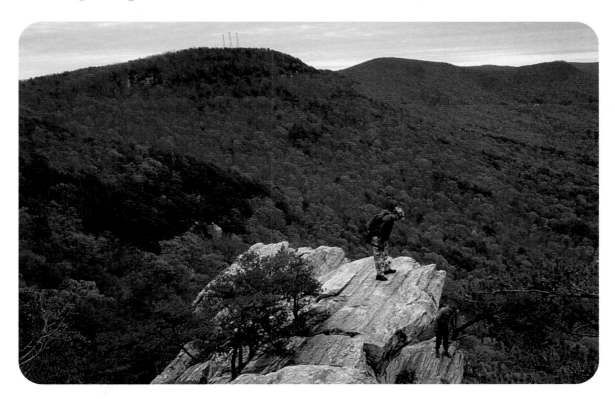

Rock climbers stare down from a granite cliff in Cheaha State Park. The cliffs are near Mount Cheaha—sometimes called Cheaha Mountain—the state's highest point.

Located in north-central Alabama, Birmingham has the highest population in the state.

to 2,408 feet, is located here in Lineville. Also found in the Piedmont Plateau are Alabama's famous marble quarries and other rock and mineral deposits, such as coal, iron, and limestone. The Piedmont Plateau is an area of hills, ridges, and valleys.

The Appalachian Ridge and Valley Region

Just north of the Piedmont is the Appalachian Ridge and Valley Region where more deposits of coal, iron ore, and limestone are found. These minerals make up the ingredients for steel, which is produced in Alabama's steel mills. The southernmost tip of the Appalachian Mountains is located in this region. The Appalachian Mountains are a chain of mountains that run from Alabama to Maine.

The Cumberland Plateau

The Cumberland Plateau lies in the northeastern corner of Alabama. A plateau is kind of like a flat-top mountain. So although the land in this area is relatively flat, in some places it still rises to about 1,800 feet.

The bodies of water in this area, such as Guntersville Lake, support almost one hundred different types of fish. There are many caves here, too, which are great habitats for different varieties of bats. Two of Alabama's most famous caves are Cathedral and Rickwood Caverns.

Many Alabama residents and visitors enjoy exploring the state's caves and caverns.

The Interior Low Plateau

The Interior Low Plateau lies in the northernmost part of the state. There the land is made up mostly of limestone, which is a whitish-colored rock usually made from the remains of ancient sea creatures. Fed by the Tennessee River, the fertile valleys in this section are ideal for farmers. Farms and ranches in the region raise cattle and other livestock and grow crops such as corn and cotton. Huntsville and Decatur are the biggest Alabama cities in this area.

The Waterways

Most of Alabama's major rivers run in a north-to-south direction and drain into the Gulf of Mexico. The one exception is the Tennessee River, which is located in the northern part of the state. The Tennessee runs east to west. The Mobile, Alabama and Tombigbee rivers are three of the most important rivers in the state. The Alabama River flows from Montgomery and meets the Tombigbee to form the Mobile River just north of the city of Mobile.

There are no large naturally occurring lakes in Alabama. But human-made dams on some of the state's rivers have created artificial lakes, such as Guntersville Lake on the Tennessee River. Damming of the Coosa River has formed Weiss, Lay, Mitchell, Jordan, and Logan Martin lakes.

At the southwestern tip of the state you can enjoy the warm waters of the Gulf of Mexico. Alabama's only

Alabama has more than 900 square miles of inland water in the form of rivers and artificial lakes. There are twenty-six rivers in Alabama. The longest ones are the 400-mile-long Tombigbee River and the 300-mile-long Alabama River.

Barrier islands can be found off the shores of Alabama's Gulf coast.

outlet to the Gulf of Mexico is along Mobile Bay. The state's coastline on the Gulf is about 50 miles long. But when you add the coastlines that occur along Mobile Bay and other smaller inlets in the area, Alabama's shoreline measures more than 600 miles.

Alabama's beaches are affected by erosion, which is the wearing away of land. Over time, wind and the Gulf's waves have eaten away at the coast. In an effort to protect the shoreline, large chunks of cement have been dropped into the water. This has created artificial reefs, where fish can hide. These reefs have increased the number of fish that live along the Gulf shores. The new reefs also help to extend and protect the shoreline.

The Climate

Alabamians enjoy a subtropical climate, which means they experience short, mild winters and long, warm summers. In winter, the average high temperature ranges between the mid-forties to the mid-fifties, depending on the elevation of the land. People living at higher elevations will have cooler weather than those living closer to sea level. During the summer, temperatures are usually in the eighties. Very low or very high temperatures are unusual. The highest temperature ever recorded in Alabama was 112 degrees Fahrenheit on September 5, 1925, in Centreville. The record low temperature was -27 degrees Fahrenheit at New Market on January 30, 1966.

Thunderstorms are common in Alabama, especially in the southern parts of the state, where the warm air from the Gulf of Mexico mixes with the cooler air from the north. In the summer, Alabamians see a lot of rain, which ranges from 53 to 68 inches each year. Large storms, such as hurricanes and tornadoes, sometimes cross Alabama, causing flooding and very strong winds.

Sometimes snow falls in the winter, but usually only in the northern mountains. In March of 1993, a storm crossed the state, causing a surprising 24 inches of snow to fall all over northern Alabama.

Wild Life

Alabama is home to a large number of different plants. Some of the most common trees include oak, hickory, magnolia, elm, ash, pine, and maple. There are trees that produce flowers, trees that are used for lumber, and trees that produce food. The most popular trees that bear nuts include the pecan and the black walnut. There are also trees that have medicinal use and are used to make people feel better. Sassafras is one example. Native Americans in the region made teas and liquid medicines from the roots of the tree.

Many different flowers grow in the state, but Alabama is most famous for its variety of azaleas. There are also many different varieties of wild flowers, which you may see growing along the roadsides, in the prairies and mountains, and even in the backyards of many Alabamians.

Because Alabama has a lot of undisturbed or undeveloped land, there are a lot of wild animals in the state. Raccoons, foxes, squirrels, deer, and rabbits can be

Alabama's warm weather is perfect for growing a number of different plants.

found in Alabama's forests. There are also many larger animals, such as bobcats and bears. Beavers make their homes near Alabama's waterways.

Alabama's rivers, lakes, and streams are home to a variety of freshwater fish. These include bass, sunfish, pikes, eels, catfish, and perch. All of these fish provide food for Alabama's large wildlife, but they also attract human fishermen. It is not uncommon to see fishermen casting their lines in the early morning or early evening.

The state's coastal waters are also filled with aquatic life. Red snapper and grouper are types of fish that live on the coastal reefs. Other sea creatures, such as crabs, oysters, and shrimp, thrive in the Gulf's salty waters.

White egrets wade in Alabama's marshes.

Many birds make their homes in Alabama. Some live there throughout the year, while others migrate to Alabama to stay warm during the winter. Birds in the Heart of Dixie include cardinals, wrens, bluebirds, martins, hummingbirds, eagles, and hawks. Waterbirds such as ducks, loons, and herons can be found in or around the state's lakes and rivers. On the coast, Alabamians may see pelicans and cormorants. Because of the variety of birds in the state, Alabama is a favorite place for bird watchers.

Protecting Alabama

As in other states, Alabama has many endangered and threatened plants and animals. Wildlife becomes threatened or endangered when habitats are lost, mostly through human interference like cutting down forests or using land for buildings. Pollution also affects wild animal populations, either directly hurting the animals or hurting the food the animals eat. Government officials, scientists, and regular Alabama citizens are working hard to keep these animals from becoming extinct or completely disappearing.

One example of an endangered species in Alabama is the gray bat. Gray bats live in caves throughout Alabama, with the largest populations found in the northern part of the state. The bats choose caves that are close to rivers or lakes because their

An American alligator rests near a lake in Eufaula. Alabamians are trying to find ways to live peacefully with all of the state's native wildlife, before more plants and animals become endangered.

diet is made up of insects that live on or near water. Cutting down trees around caves takes away the protective covering that gray bats need to fly safely to and from the water. In recent years, the loss of habitat has caused gray bats to be put on the Endangered Species list.

In the past, Alabama was not known for its environmental protection programs, but that has changed. Over time, Alabamians have become more informed about keeping the state's water clean and protecting all the wild creatures—right down to the tiny beach mouse. Around the state, many organizations have been established to keep the natural beauty of Alabama alive. Groups of volunteers have come together to protect the state's wildflowers, the great rivers, the lush forests, and the coastal beaches. Alabamians are working hard. They know they live in a wonderful state, and they want to keep it that way.

Plants & Animals

Wild Turkey

At one time, the number of wild turkeys living in Alabama was very low. But Alabamians have worked to bring this large bird back. Wild turkeys are one of the biggest birds in North America and can grow to be 4 feet long from head to tail. But even though the wild turkey is big, it is a fast flier, especially over short distances, and sometimes can go as fast as 55 miles per hour.

Eastern Diamondback Rattlesnake

Alabama is home to many different kinds of rattlesnakes, but the Eastern diamondback is one of the largest. It can grow to be 8 feet long. This rattler likes the dry, flat land in pine forests, where it survives on mice, rats, rabbits, and sometimes birds.

White-Tailed Deer

White-tailed deer are found all over Alabama, even in or near major cities. When the deer are young fawns, they have white spots on their sides. This helps them hide from danger. As they grow, the spots disappear and their coats are mostly brown. The deer's keen sense of smell and its sharp sense of hearing help to keep it out of danger.

Black Bear

It is uncertain how many wild black bears still live in Alabama. Scientists have seen bears in some of the swamplands, but they are not yet sure if the bears are just passing through the state or if they live there. Black bears usually stand between 4 and 7 feet tall. Adult males can weigh as much as 500 pounds. Black bears eat plants, berries, nuts, fruits, and insects.

Poison Ivy

Poison ivy is found throughout much of North America. In Alabama, the plant's berries are the yellowhammer's favorite food. Humans should try to stay away from poison ivy because it can cause painful and very itchy skin problems. Oils—which are found on all parts of the plant—cause the skin problems. Poison ivy can be identified by its glossy three-leafed form.

Goldenrod

At one time goldenrod was the state flower of Alabama. It is a very common wild flower with many different varieties. But all goldenrod plants have long spikes of bright yellow flowers. Goldenrods attract butterflies, and many Alabamians plant the flowers in their gardens to attract these pretty insects.

2 From the Beginning

The First Residents

The first people to live in the land now called Alabama are often called Paleo-Indians. Scientists have estimated these early inhabitants may have lived here as many as 9,000 years ago. It is believed they originally came from Asia to North America across a land bridge between the two continents that no longer exists.

Paleo-Indians may have first reached the region that includes Alabama around 7000 BCE. They made homes in the many limestone caves here. The caves sheltered them from the rain and the cold in winter and kept them cool in summer. The thick forests and clear rivers provided them with food. They hunted bear and deer, gathered nuts and fruits, and caught fish and turtles.

Russell Cave, located in northeast Alabama, has provided archaeologists (scientists who study ancient artifacts and cultures) with evidence that ancient people lived there for at least 8,000 years. The archaeologists have uncovered tools, pottery, weapons, and bones.

In the early 1920s, whole Alabama families—including children—had to work to make a living.

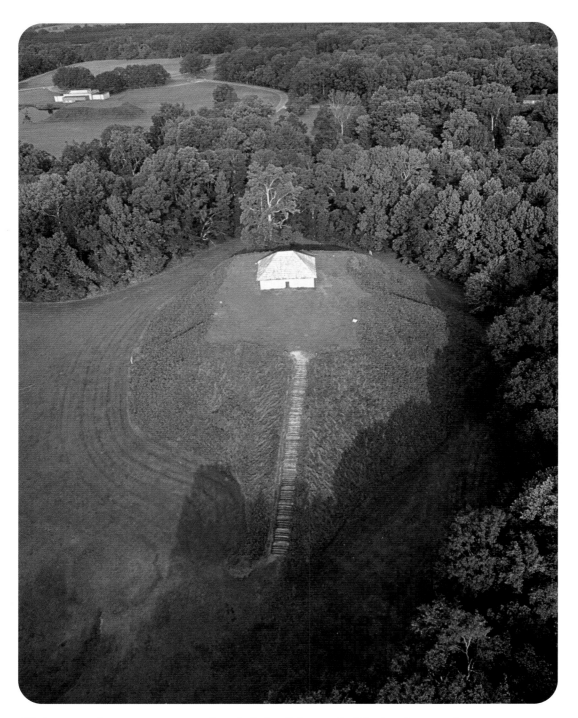

Visitors to the state can see what is left of the early Natives' mounds at Moundville Park.

Alabama

Several thousand years later, the Native people living in the region built large mounds. Scientists and historians today often call these people Mound Builders. Some Native groups built homes on top of the mounds. Other groups built religious temples or used the mounds as sacred burial places. Then, about six hundred years later, the Mound Builders disappeared. No one knows for sure what happened to them. They may have been killed by a deadly disease. It is also possible that they ran out of food and moved to another region. Today some of the mounds still exist in many states. In Alabama mounds still exist in Hale County, Baldwin County, and Dauphin Island.

The Creek Confederacy

Many years after the Mound Builders disappeared, new groups of Native people began living in the region. Although these bands of Natives each had their own name, Europeans who came to the area referred to them as the Creeks. The Creeks formed a larger group in order to protect themselves from the European invaders. This group was called the Creek Confederacy. The Confederacy was made up of more than seventeen different Native groups that spoke the same language, which was called Muskogean.

The Creeks were farmers. They grew corn, beans, and squash and raised cows, pigs, and horses. They lived in well-organized villages. Each community had its own leaders who met every day to discuss problems and solutions. The Creeks also liked to have fun. One of their favorite activities

The name *Creek* was given by the British to the Native Americans in living in the region. The British chose this name because these Natives always built their villages on the banks of creeks, which are small branches of major rivers.

was a game called chunkey. It was played with spears, which were thrown at a round rock. Foot races were another popular activity.

Although the Creeks fought with the earliest European explorers, they learned to trust later settlers and even offered food to prevent European settlers from starving. The Creeks were very generous. They welcomed strangers to their villages and eventually adjusted to many of the European customs. Many Creeks even married Europeans.

The Spanish Explorers

The coastline of present-day Alabama was searched by Europeans early in the sixteenth century, but no one is certain of the exact date. Historians do know, however, that the outline of Mobile Bay first appeared on a map of North America in 1505. But it was not until 1519 that an official visit was recorded. Spain's Alonso Álvarez de Pineda sailed into Mobile Bay but did not stay there very long.

In 1539, Hernando de Soto, the governor of Cuba, landed in what is now Tampa Bay, Florida. He had with him a well-armed group of about seven hundred men. First, De Soto marched his men to what is now Tennessee, and then he turned south and entered the area of present-day Alabama. De Soto was looking for gold. When he could not find it, he went into Native American villages, forced his way into their homes, and stole anything of value. De Soto and his men also often beat and tortured the Native people if they did not follow his orders. His men stole the Native American's food and horses. Word of De Soto's bad reputation began to spread throughout the different Native groups, and eventually the Natives decided to fight back.

Some of the Native American villages that De Soto visited may have looked like this one, which was located near Malvilla.

In October 1540, a chief named Tuscaloosa planned a surprise attack on De Soto's army. The battle at Mabila did not go well for Tuscaloosa's men. Most of them were killed alongside many soldiers in Soto's army. Although De Soto won this battle, he decided to leave the area because his surviving soldiers were badly wounded.

It would take almost twenty years before another group of Spanish explorers entered the region again. Tristán de Luna came with settlers who tried to establish a colony near Mobile Bay. De Luna was also looking for gold. Like De Soto before him,

De Luna did not find it. Many of his people died from disease or hunger. So after three years, the Spanish colony was abandoned.

The French Colonists

In 1689, the explorer René-Robert Cavelier, Sieur de La Salle, traveled down the Mississippi River and claimed for France all the land around the Mississippi River. This included present-day Alabama. He named the land the Louisiana Territory. Ten years later, in 1699, two brothers, Pierre and Jean-Baptiste Le Moyne landed on Dauphin Island in Mobile Bay, ready to take on their jobs as governors of the Territory.

By 1702, the first permanent, white settlement in Alabama was established at the mouth of Mobile Bay. But life was not easy. There was very little food and there were many diseases. Added to this were constant battles with pirates and Spanish settlers who still lingered in the area.

These early French settlers tried hard to raise crops, but they found that they needed a lot more help with the labor. So they brought over about six hundred slaves—the first black slaves to enter the region. But even this extra help did not save the settlers. The French might have starved to death if the Creeks had not shared their food with them.

The French finally found they could make more money selling furs from wild animals, such as beavers. Unfortunately, British fur trappers were moving into the area, and the competition for the land and the fur trade grew very serious. The dispute over who had the right to hunt on the land erupted into what would be called the French and Indian Wars. Many Native Americans sided with the French as they fought the British. But the French were defeated and had to sign the Treaty of

Paris of 1763. This forced the French to surrender all their land in the region, which included present-day Alabama. The British now controlled the region.

Statehood

After winning the French and Indian Wars, the British controlled the area of Alabama for fewer than twenty years. In the late 1770s, the British colonies on the Atlantic coast went to war for their independence from Great Britain. The colonists won the Revolutionary War and the new government signed another Treaty of Paris in 1783. The victory over Great Britain gave the newly formed United States the right to the land east of the Mississippi River. But Spain argued against this claim, stating that they still owned the southern coastline around Mobile. The United States did not have full control over the region. It was not until the end of the War of 1812 (fought between Great Britain and the United States) that the United States government finally gained control of all the land that today includes Alabama.

In 1817, the land was named the Territory of Alabama. Two years after that, Alabama become a state. Alabama was fully admitted to the United

Andrew Dexter was one of the founders of the city of Montgomery, which would eventually become Alabama's capital.

States on December 14, 1819. The new state's legislators—or lawmakers—first met in Huntsville. Cahaba was the next city to serve as Alabama's capital, until 1826 when Tuscaloosa was chosen. Montgomery was voted as the new state capital in 1846, and is still Alabama's capital city today.

By the 1850s, Alabama's economy was booming, mostly because of cotton. People from all over the states came to Alabama, and many brought hundreds of slaves with them. This brought prosperity to Alabama, but it also brought problems.

As more settlers and farmers arrived, pressure was put on the Native groups to give up their land. Unfair treaties between the United States and Native Americans were written. The Natives were often forced to sign the treaties, and in many cases, the United States did not keep their promises. Most of the Native Americans who had once lived in Alabama were forced to move. Tens of thousands were sent west to Indian Territory, which was located in present-day Oklahoma. One of the most famous forced-removals of Native Americans was called the Trail of Tears. In 1838, thousands of Native Americans—mostly Cherokee—had to abandon their homes. They were forced to march west for more than 1,000 miles. During the march, almost 4,000 Native Americans died from cold, hunger, or disease.

The Trail of Tears was roughly on the route that is now Highway 72 in the northern part of Alabama, going from Bridgeport, in the east, to Waterloo, in the west.

Cotton plantations in the South were dependent on slave labor. Without the workers, the crops could not be harvested.

Civil War and Reconstruction

By 1860, Alabama was producing a record amount of cotton. In order to handle all the labor, Alabama's farmers bought thousands of slaves. So many slaves lived in the state during this time that Alabama's black population almost equaled the white population. When Abraham Lincoln—who was in favor of abolishing or ending slavery—was elected president, many people in Alabama and other Southern states were upset. Part of the reason was because they did not want to lose their slaves. Slave

Make a Sachet

Alabama's residents often used chests to store such things as clothes and blankets. To keep things smelling fresh, they often used sachets—cloth pouches filled with fragrant plants such as herbs or flowers. Follow these instructions to make your own sachet.

What You Need

2 pieces of cotton fabric-each piece must be 3 inches
    by 4 inches
Pins
Scissors
Sewing needle
Thread
Narrow ribbon, about 5 or 6 inches long

Put one fabric piece on top of the other, with the outsides (or printed sides) facing each other. Pin the edges together on three sides.

Cut an 18-inch piece of thread and carefully thread it through the needle. Knot the end of the thread.

Using the needle and thread, stitch around the three pinned sides. You might need an adult to help you with the sewing. After your last stitch, make a knot in the thread and cut off the extra thread.

Carefully remove the pins and put them in a safe place where no one will get pricked.

Gently turn the pouch right-side out.

To make the sachet smell nice fill it half-full with potpourri. If you do not have potpourri, you can also stuff the sachet with scented dryer sheets or with cotton balls that have been lightly sprayed with a favorite perfume or cologne.

Tie the sachet closed using the ribbon. You can use your sachet to make your clothes smell nice or give it as a gift.

This illustration from 1861 shows crowds gathered in Montgomery to watch Jefferson Davis being inaugurated as president of the Confederacy.

labor was necessary for Southern plantations to be successful. Southern states made plans to secede or break away from the United States.

In 1861, leaders from the Southern states met in Montgomery and created a new nation called the Confederate States of America. Montgomery was the Confederacy's capital. Jefferson Davis, former U.S. Senator from Mississippi, was elected president of the Confedercy.

Alabama

One year later, war broke out between Confederate soldiers and Union—or Northern—forces. Not all Alabamians favored the Confederacy. Some Alabamians did not believe in slavery. These people either hid in the northern hills of Alabama and refused to fight or they joined the Union armies. Also, many slaves managed to run away, and some of them also joined the Northern forces.

There were no major battles fought on Alabamian soil. However, Union forces occupied several Alabama cities and Alabamian homes and lives were lost during the Civil War.

The Battle of Mobile Bay was an important victory for the Union.

There was a big fight in Mobile Bay because it was an important port through which the Confederate forces received supplies. The Union knew they had to take control of this port, so they fought the Confederate forces and won in 1864. A year later, the Civil War ended and the South admitted defeat.

Life was not easy after the Civil War for white or black people in the South. There was a shortage of food, farms and crops had been destroyed, and there were not many jobs available. Even though freed slaves enjoyed privileges they had never been given before, they did not enjoy them for very long. The Alabama government had signed the fourteenth amendment to the U.S. Constitution, which guaranteed equal protection under the law to all citizens, including freed slaves. But Alabama created its own state laws that took away many rights from African Americans. Reconstruction—the rebuilding of the South—helped Alabama recover from the war, and life in Alabama was slowly improving, but not all of Alabama's citizens were benefiting from these changes.

A system of laws was passed in many Southern states after the Civil War that severely limited the legal rights of freed slaves. These laws were referred to as the Black Code and included restrictions on the rights of African Americans to vote and to hold political office.

Much of Alabama's cotton was sent to the state's textile mills. At the mills, the fiber was used to make clothing, blankets, and other material.

Changing Times

Farming continued to be a major source of income for many Alabamians at the end of the 1800s. But the processing of iron in northeastern Alabama created new jobs and a new city. Birmingham, located in the heart of the mining lands, was founded in 1871.

Another important industry at this time was cotton textiles. Cotton textiles were used to make things like sheets, clothing, and towels. Railroads, which had been built during Reconstruction, helped Alabama's industries by providing transportation for goods. The products were taken from the factories to other cities or to Mobile Bay, where they were shipped out of the state.

Men and boys of all ages worked in Alabama's mines. In the early 1900s, Alabama's mined material were mostly used for suppplies for the war efforts.

During the first half of the twentieth century, an insect called the boll weevil destroyed much of Alabama's cotton crops. New food crops, such as peanuts, were planted. This helped to save many people from having to close down their farms. Alabama's economy was also helped when the United States entered World War I. American factories and farms produced supplies that the troops needed during the war.

In 1929, however, the American economy took a downward turn. The Great Depression hit the country and many stores and banks went out of business. Most Americans lost their jobs. Farms failed and had to be closed down. Many Alabamians left the state to look for jobs. The United States government did what it could to help the people, establishing make-work programs

Alabama

throughout the country. These programs created jobs that had the workers building and repairing roads and bridges, or working in lumber mills in the nation's forests.

One of Alabama's nicknames is the Heart of Dixie. The word *Dixie* is a nickname for the South. In the 1940s and 1950s, Alabamians decided to promote their state as the center—or the heart—of the South.

The United States entered World War II in 1941, and this also helped the country's economy. Factories and farms again had to provide needed supplies for American troops. States' economies—including Alabama's—improved.

Alabama's cities, such as Montgomery, continued to grow in the 1950s and 1960s.

In the 1950s, a new industry brought prosperity to parts of Alabama. Huntsville became an important center for rocket and space research. This industry created more jobs for Alabamians. For example, the Saturn V rocket was developed at NASA's (National Aeronautics and Space Administration's) Space Flight Center in Huntsville. In 1969, a Saturn V rocket propelled *Apollo 11* into space, where Neil Armstrong became the first man to walk on the moon.

Around the same time the space program was developing, African Americans began fighting for their civil rights. They had grown tired of being denied the same rights as white citizens. They fought against segregation, which was a system that separated whites from blacks. Because of segregation, African Americans could not shop at some stores, could not eat at certain restaurants and had to sit in the backs of public buses. Many African Americans could only hold low-paying jobs because they were not given better opportunities. Black children could not attend the same schools as white children, and the all-black schools were not given enough government money and did not have the same programs or supplies as white schools. In many cases, African Americans in parts of the United States still did not have the right to vote.

As a result of Rosa Parks' brave actions, the Supereme Court decided that segregation on Montgomery's city buses was illegal.

The Civil Rights Movement, in which many African Americans and whites led peaceful marches and protests, was very active in Alabama. In 1955, Rosa Parks refused to go to the back of a Montgomery City bus to give up her seat to a white man. She was arrested for this, which led to the Montgomery bus boycott. During the boycott, Alabama citizens—black and white—who opposed segregation refused to use Montgomery's buses. In 1956, the United States Supreme Court—the highest court in the country—declared segregated bus seating illegal. This marked the beginning of the Civil Rights Movement.

Martin Luther King Jr., a pastor of a church in Montgomery, brought the hardships of everyday life of blacks to the attention of

In this photograph, Martin Luther King Jr. and his wife, Coretta Scott King, are marching with other civil rights activists though a neighborhood in Selma in 1965.

people throughout the United States and the world. In 1965, Dr. King led one of the most significant marches in the fight for civil rights. This march began in Selma and ended in Montgomery, 80 miles away. The people in this march were fighting for African Americans' right to vote. It would be a long hard battle, but eventually African Americans would gain their equal rights.

Modern Alabama

From the end of the twentieth century and into the beginning of the twenty-first century, Alabama has undergone some changes. The population increased and new residents began living in different parts of the state. In the early 1900s, most Alabamians lived in rural communities and held jobs related to farming and agriculture. But during the last half of the century, more than 60 percent of the population moved to the cities or the areas right outside the cities. This was a major shift for Alabama, which had been previously been a very rural state. From 1970 on, people were moving off their farms in increasing numbers. The settled in the cities to find jobs nonagricultural jobs, such as those in manufacturing and social services.

This caused an increase in suburban areas around Alabama's larger cities. Many counties around Alabama's cities doubled in population. Counties with a more rural setting lost half or more of the people who used to live there. Instead of being spread out throughout the state, people were living in clusters in urban areas. While this was good for the cities' economies, this also meant that problems such as air pollution, traffic jams, and the need for larger schools became worse. Meanwhile, the rural areas were facing a rise in poverty as fewer people left the region, causing stores and businesses to close.

When Hurricane Katrina struck land in 2005, many Gulf Coastal states—including Alabama—were hit hard. The hurricane caused millions of dollars in damage and many homes and lives were lost.

Today, people are searching for solutions to help the rural counties find ways to make money and to keep Alabama's city dwellers' environment clean and safe. Officials are trying to attract new industries to provide more jobs both in the urban and rural areas. Other people are focusing on how to adjust to the swiftly growing cities.

Although the twenty-first century is bringing a lot of change to Alabama, people who live here still enjoy some of the same things that have always made Alabama a great state. There are still thousands of acres of well-preserved forests and many

Young people have an opportunity to learn about spacecraft at the United States Space Camp in Huntsvillle.

miles of rivers. Alabama farmers can still make a living on the fertile soil by growing cotton and peanuts and raising livestock. Birmingham remains a major, city not only in producing steel, but also in providing services for all the people of this state. And in Huntsville, which has been nicknamed Rocket City, U.S.A., scientists continue to research better equipment for America's space program. Alabama is growing in many different ways, and its people are hard at work to make sure those changes are for the better.

Alabama

Important Dates

10,000 to 7000 BCE   Paleo-Indians live in Alabama's caves.

700 to 1300 CE   Modern Native culture develops, including the groups such as the Creek.

1519   Alonso Álvarez de Pineda becomes first European to enter Mobile Bay.

1540   Hernando de Soto explores Alabama in search of gold.

1559   Tristán de Luna builds a temporary settlement in Mobile Bay.

1689   Explorer La Salle, travels down the Mississippi River and claims all the and around the Mississippi River, including present-day Alabama, for France.

1702   The first permanent non-Native settlement is established at Mobile Bay.

1763   The French are defeated and sign the Treaty of Paris of 1763. They lose their rights to land that includes present-day Alabama.

1817   Alabama becomes an official territory of the United States.

1819   Alabama becomes a state on December 14.

1850s   Cotton becomes an important crop for the state.

1861   Alabama votes to secede from the Union and joins the Confederacy.

1865   The Civil War ends and Alabama rejoins the Union.

1955   Rosa Parks refuses to sit at the back of the bus and the Montgomery bus boycott begins.

1965   Reverend Martin Luther King Jr. leads a protest march from Selma to Montgomery.

2001   Condoleezza Rice, born in Birmingham, becomes the first woman to ever hold the office of National Security Advisor.

2002   Birmingham native Vonetta Flowers wins a gold medal in bobsledding, becoming the first African American to win a gold medal in the Winter Olympics.

2005   Hurricane Katrina causes widespread damage along the Alabama coast.

2006   Scientists at Huntsville's Marshall Space Flight Center announce that they will take part in the building of a new series of rockets and a lunar lander that will be sent to the moon.

De Soto

Cotton crops

3 The People

Since the Civil War, the population of Alabama has grown from more than one million to more than four million people. Throughout this time, the state has seen many changes. People from other parts of the country and from around the world have made Alabama their home. Residents have moved from rural areas to urban areas, causing Alabama's cities and suburbs to grow and expand. Today, most Alabamians live in the state's largest cities, which include Birmingham, Mobile, Huntsville, Montgomery, Tuscaloosa, Florence, Anniston, and Gadsden.

The largest portion of Alabama's population is Caucasian or white. Around 71 percent of the state's residents are of European descent. (This includes people of French, British, German, and Portuguese ancestry, to name just a few.) Some residents are immigrants from those countries, while others may have parents, grandparents, or ancestors from Europe. Several Alabamian families can trace their roots

Colorful flowers bloom outside an Civil War-Era mansion in Eufala.
Alabamians have called the state their home for nearly two hundred years.

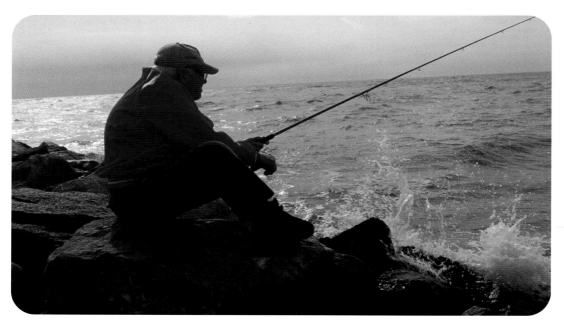

Some Alabamians are descended from the first European settlers to make their homes in the region.

all the way back to European settlers who first came to the region, more than one hundred years ago.

Influences from these different European cultures can be found not only in Alabama's people but also in the architecture (the buildings), in cultural events, and in the names of towns and counties throughout the state. For example, Alabama's French culture is reflected in Mobile's celebration of Mardi Gras. The Creole culture, which is a mixture of French, African, and Native American cultures, is also present in Alabama. There are Alabamians of Creole descent, and several restaurants in the state serve traditional Creole food.

Place names in Alabama also reflect the state's European ancestry. For example, Cullman County was named after John G. Cullman, a German immigrant who settled in northern Alabama and encouraged other Germans to follow him.

Native Americans

From 10,000 BCE to 7000 BCE the Paleo-Indians were the first people to live in Alabama. Many of these people did not build permanent homes, but instead traveled with the seasons in search of food. Around 1000 BCE, the descendants of these early peoples had lifestyles that were different. These Natives started to build permanent settlements. They planted crops and for hunting, used bows and arrows—tools that the earliest of the Paleo-Indians did not have.

Thousands of years later, Native life changed even more. Native groups started working and living close together to improve their hunting success. Organized communities and settlements were developed. But in the 1500s, the Natives were introduced to European influences. As Europeans came to search for gold or explore the land, many Natives were killed by the diseases the Europeans carried or in battles against the newcomers.

When the Europeans returned to the Alabama area in 1700 to try to create permanent settlements, the largest Native group they found there was the Muskogee, who were also known as the Creeks. But by 1814, the Creeks had signed away most of their land to the United States government through many treaties. Most of the Native Americans were then forcibly removed from Alabama. A few Alabamian Natives escaped this removal plan. One of these groups is the Poarch Band of the Creeks.

Today there are 2,200 members of the Poarch Band of Creeks who still live on their land about sixty miles northeast of Mobile. But the Poarch-Creeks are not the only Native people still living in Alabama. About .5 percent of the state's total population is of Native American heritage. That equals about 22,000 Native American Alabamians make their homes throughout the state. Some live and work in rural communities, while others run businesses or have jobs in the cities.

Latinos

Although explorers from Spain were the first white people to land on the soil of Alabama, people who are from Spain or have Spanish ancestors make up a very small portion of the population. However, a growing minority are the Latino people. These are residents whose families are from Mexico, Cuba,

The growth of Alabama's cities, like Birmingham, encouraged more people from different parts of the country—and the world—to move to the Heart of Dixie.

Puerto Rico, and other countries in Central and South America. Sometimes these residents are also called Hispanic Americans, and they make up about 2.2 percent of the population.

In the past ten years, however, the population of Latino Alabamians has grown more than any other minority group. Many Latinos have come to the state to attend the schools, or work and own successful businesses. Several Latino families have been living in Alabama for decades. Some experts are predicting that in the future, there will be more Hispanics and Latinos than African Americans living in Alabama.

Asian Americans

Less than 1 percent of Alabama's population is Asian or Asian American. Some of the countries from which these Alabama citizens or their ancestors have come include Vietnam, Japan, China, Laos, the Philippines, and Cambodia. There are some Asian Americans who have lived in Alabama for many generations, while others have arrived only recently. Much of Alabama's Asian-American population is concentrated in counties such as Madison, Mobile, Lee, Dale, and Tuscaloosa.

Asian Americans make up a small but important part of Alabama's population.

Famous Alabamians

Helen Keller: Speaker and Author

Helen Keller was born in 1880 in Tuscumbia. At an early age, Helen lost her sight and hearing. Despite her inability to see or hear, Helen graduated with honors from Radcliffe College. Keller spent much of her life trying to help others—especially people with disabilities or people who did not have equal rights. She became a famous writer and speaker and traveled around the world.

W.C. Handy: Musician

W.C. Handy was born in Florence in 1873 and was involved in music throughout his life. Whether he was playing or writing music, he worked on creating a new style. He wrote more than 150 different compositions, including the famous "St. Louis Blues." Handy had lost his eyesight by the time he was forty, but this did not stop him from writing and performing his music. W.C. Handy died in 1958 and is often called the Father of the Blues.

N. Jan Davis: Scientist and Astronaut

N. Jan Davis was born in Florida, but moved with her family to Huntsville at an early age and thinks of Huntsville as her hometown. After receiving a degree in mechanical engineering and science from the University of Alabama, she worked for NASA's Marshall Space Flight Center in Huntsville. In 1992, Dr. Davis was assigned as a mission specialist on the Space Shuttle's fiftieth mission. She spent eight days in space in the Spacelab. For her work in space, she received the NASA Exceptional Service Medal.

Rosa Parks: Civil Rights Activist

A native of Tuskegee, Rosa Parks is often called the Mother of the Civil Rights Movement. She was very active in fighting for equal rights for African Americans and is best remembered for refusing to give up her seat on a bus. Her action led to a citywide boycott of Montgomery's buses. The boycott, in turn, triggered widespread protests against segregation all across the United States. Rosa Parks died in 2005.

Jesse Owens: Olympic Athlete

In 1913, Jesse Owens was born in Danville. A strong athlete throughout his younger years, when he was only twenty-two years old, Owens set three world records in the 220-yard low hurdles race and in the broad jump. He qualified for the 1936 Olympics, in which he also set records in the 100-meter race and in the broad jump. Jesse Owens became the fourth American to win three or more gold medals in the Olympic Games. Owens' triumphs were especially notable because he lived during a time when African Americans had very few rights and privileges. In 1976, Owens was awarded the Medal of Freedom—one of the nations' highest honors. He died in 1980.

Harper Lee: Author

Nelle Harper Lee was born in 1926 born in Monroeville. She is best known for her Pulitzer Prize-wining novel, To Kill a Mockingbird, *which has been called one of the most important books of the twentieth century. Her novel tells the story of an African-American man who is wrongly accused of a crime, the white lawyer who defends him, and the relationship between the lawyer and his children. The story is set in Alabama and more than ten million copies of the novel have been sold all over the world.*

African Americans

In 1721, aboard the ship the *Africane*, more than one hundred black slaves were delivered to their Alabama owners. Later, as the cotton crop gained importance to the Alabama economy, more slaves entered the state. By the middle of the nineteenth century, there were almost a half a million slaves living in the state. But not all blacks in Alabama were slaves. There was also a small population of freed slaves.

After the end of the Civil War, all slaves were freed, but many of them continued to live close to their former owners, who gave them land on which to plant crops. But there was a catch to this plan. These freed slaves, who were called share-croppers, had to give the landowners a large portion of the food they raised as a form of rent payment for this land. In many instances, they were allowed to keep only enough food to eat, and had none left over to sell for extra money.

One of the main problems for blacks living in the South was segregation, which prevented them from doing many things that white people were allowed to do. Through the efforts of people like Dr. Martin Luther King Jr. and members of such groups as the National Association for the Advancement of Colored People (NAACP), African Americans finally won their civil rights as segregation was made illegal.

Many African Americans still make their homes in Alabama, and represent the largest

Booker T. Washington, a freed slave, tried to change the poor conditions in which most African Americans lived in Alabama. He started a school for blacks—the only one of its kind in the United States at that time. The school, founded in 1881, was called the Tuskegee Institute.

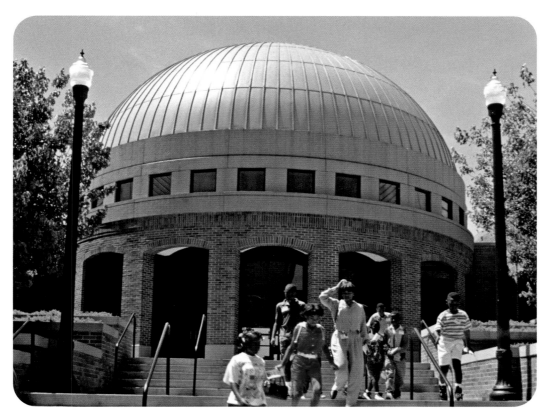

Schoolchildern visit the Civil Rights Institute in Birmingham to learn about the history of the Civil Rights movement in the United States.

minority in the state—about 26 percent of the population. Like all state residents, African-American Alabamians play an important part in the state's history, economy, and culture. African Americans from Alabama have made many contributions to the country in a variety of professional fields. Condoleeza Rice was the first woman to serve as the country's National Security Advisor. Mae Jemison was the first African American woman astronaut. In professional basketball, Leeds native Charles Barkley was an impressive athlete. In the entertainment industry, Nell Carter from Birmingham was an award-winning actress and singer who became famous on television and on Broadway.

Young Alabamians sing traditional songs that honor the state's past. Music has a long history in Alabama.

No matter where Alabamians come from, one thing many people in the state seem to have in common is a love of music. Alabama is home to hundreds of musicians and musical festivals. Musicians in Alabama are said to be greatly responsible for developing both blues and country music. But you can also find zydeco, or Cajun, music from the French Creole people, German polkas, Appalachian fiddling, Hispanic mariachi, American rock and roll, and African-American-inspired jazz and soul. Alabama is also famous for producing music stars such as Nat King Cole, Hank Williams, Lionel Ritchie, Emmylou Harris, and the Temptations.

Alabama is and has been home to famous people, such as entertainers, politicians, and civil rights leaders, to everyday Alabamians like school teachers, bank tellers, and store owners.

Alabama

The Heart of Dixie is filled with people from all different backgrounds, working together to make Alabama a great state.

Alabama residents may be descended from people who settled the land hundreds of years ago, or they may have moved to the state more recently. They may come from different cultures, but Alabamians from a variety of ethnic backgrounds love their state. Some may live in their same hometown all their lives, while others might travel far away. No matter where Alabamians live, no matter how far away some might roam, Alabama will always be where their hearts are.

Calendar of Events

Mardi Gras in Mobile

In February, Alabama celebrates Mardi Gras. The mostly outdoor festival stretches over a two-week period with parades and lots of activities for people of all ages.

Rattlesnake Rodeo

The town of Opp may not be Alabama's most famous city except in March when the Rattlesnake Rodeo is held. This celebration first started out in 1959 as a snake roundup. Today, it has grown to include dancing contests, performances, arts and crafts, and a lot of great food to enjoy.

Dogwood Festival

Athens sponsors a Dogwood Festival in April to honor the pretty spring blossoms. But the Festival also has duck races, a doll show, and a concert in the park.

The Helen Keller Festival

In June, Tuscumbia honors Helen Keller with a fun festival that lasts three days. There are many activities to enjoy, such as a parade through the town, arts and crafts booths, puppet shows, and sports tournaments. You can also watch a live performance of *The Miracle Worker,* the famous play about Keller's life.

Fiddle Fest

In August, Moulton hosts a Fiddle Fest where you can watch fiddlers—from beginners to masters—compete with one another. You can also hear music played on banjos, mandolins, harmonicas, and guitars, and enjoy dancing and arts and crafts. During the festival, ceremonies are held to induct musicians into the local music hall of fame.

Dogwood blossoms

Alabama Catfish Festival

If you like fishing, especially for catfish, you might want to head to Greensboro for the Alabama Catfish Festival in September. There you can watch catfish races, a rodeo, and have fun at a children's carnival. A tour of the local fish farms is also available.

Renaissance Faire

In October, Florence puts on a Renaissance Faire to celebrate Europe's culture and history during the Middle Ages, and most fair participants are dressed in traditional clothing. At the fair, you can eat great food, listen to live music performances, and watch knights fight in mock battle.

National Peanut Festival

Dothan is known for its favorite crop, the peanut. In November the city holds a National Peanut Festival. The celebration lasts for two weeks and has a carnival, fair, parade and beauty pageant. Dothan is often called the Peanut Capital of America.

Preparing costumes for a festival

Christmas on the River

Every year in the beginning of December, tens of thousands of people come to Demopolis for their Christmas on the River celebration. The main attraction is the parade of lighted floats that drift down the river at night. But the festival also includes candlelight tours of historic homes, a children's parade, an arts and crafts show, a barbeque cook-off and fireworks displays.

4 How It Works

There are different levels of government in the Heart of Dixie. Nearly all of Alabama's towns and cities have their own local government. But they are not all alike. Some cities or towns have mayors and city councils who are elected by the residents. Other cities have a commission or a city manager. Whatever form it takes, local government is responsible for issues that are specific to the town or city. These issues may include land use, school budgets, housing plans and problems, and local law enforcement.

Alabamians also have elected officials who represent them at the national level. Alabama elects two people to serve in the U.S. Senate and seven congressmen or congresswomen who serve in the U.S. House of Representatives.

Based on where they are located, Alabama's towns and cities are grouped together into counties. The state has sixty-seven counties. County government is

The State Capitol is in Montgomery.

responsible for handling issues that affect multiple towns and cities. Elected county officials include tax assessors, boards of education, county commissioners, and certain judges.

Alabama's Constitutions

Each state in the Union has its own constitution, which is a legal document that contains a series of laws by which the

Branches of Government

Executive The governor, who is the head of the executive branch, is responsible for making sure laws are enforced. He or she can sign a law into practice or veto (reject) a law that the legislature has passed. Alabama's governor is elected into office and may serve more than one term, which means he or she can be elected into office multiple times. The executive branch also includes the state's lieutenant-governor, secretary of state, attorney general, treasurer, auditor, and commissioner of agriculture industries.

Legislative The state legislature is called the General Assembly. It is made up of two separate houses-the state senate and the state house of representatives. There are 35 senators and 105 state representatives. Each of these officials is elected into office by Alabama citizens. The legislature is responsible for creating new laws.

Judicial The judicial branch is headed by the State Supreme Court, which is the highest court in the state. This court is led by a chief justice and eight associate judges. Other lower courts include the court of civil appeals and the court of criminal appeals. The responsibility of the judicial branch is to hear trials.

state is governed. Over the years, the people in Alabama's legislature have written six different constitutions.

The first constitution was written when Alabama became a state in 1819. Then a new constitution replaced it 1861, around the time of the Civil War. A third was created after the Civil War in 1865, only to be replaced by the fourth constitution in 1868, which was written during Reconstruction. The fifth constitution was written in 1875. And finally, in 1901, the constitution that is still in use today was put into practice.

Alabama's current constitution, with all its amendments or additions, is the longest constitution in the world. It is approximately 310,000 words long, while most other state constitutions are only about 26,000 words long. Some people in Alabama think the state constitution is too long and too detailed. There are many people who are debating whether Alabama should have a new constitution. These people believe a new constitution would do things such as removing laws that allowed discrimination based on race, and changing laws so that more power would be granted to Alabama's cities.

How a Bill Becomes a Law

According to the Alabama state constitution, no law can be passed unless it first becomes a bill. A bill is a proposed law that has been written out in the proper legal form. There are steps that a bill must go through in order to become a law.

First, the bill is presented to one of the houses of the General Assembly. It is then assigned an official number. The bill is then read to the members of that house on three different occasions. The first time it is read, only the title of

Different rooms in the State Capitol hold pieces of Alabama history—from portraits to furniture used by the state's first legislators.

the bill is mentioned. Then the bill is discussed by a special committee of senators or representatives. For example, if the bill involves a state health issue, then it will be sent to the special committee who focuses on health. If the bill involves education, it will be sent to the special committee for educational issues. It is the committee's job to decide if the bill should be read for the second time in front of all the senators or representatives. Sometimes bills get no further than a committee reading. But if the committee approves the bill, the second reading is done by mentioning only the title of the bill. It is not until the third reading that the entire bill may be read to all members.

After the third reading, members of the house or senate may debate the bill and the issues it addresses. Changes can be made to the bill. When they are satisfied with the bill, the senators or representatives vote on it. Voting is done differently in the senate than in the house. Since there are only thirty-five members in the senate, most times the senators' names are called out in alphabetical order, and they give their vote out loud. The process in the house is different because there are 105 representatives, and it might take too long. So representatives vote electronically by pushing buttons located on their desks. If enough senators or representatives vote in favor of the bill, it moves to the other house. For example, if the bill was first introduced and approved in the senate, it then goes to the house of representatives.

The bill undergoes mostly the same process in the other half of the General Assembly. The bill is discussed, debated, and possibly changed. If enough officials support it is passed on to the governor for approval. If the governor approves the bill, he or she signs it into law. The governor can also veto or reject the bill. The bill can still become law if enough senators and representatives vote to override the governor.

Making a Difference

Alabama's state legislature is there to serve Alabamians. In fact, many ideas for bills or laws come from state residents. They consider issues that affect their communities and then point these issues out to their state legislators. For example, the idea to make the blackberry the official state fruit came from young students in Baldwin County. Both the senate and the house of representatives passed the bill, and in 2004 the blackberry became Alabama's state fruit.

To find out more about Alabama's legislature, go to this Web site http://www.legislature.state.al.us/

5 Making a Living

Agriculture

Alabama has long been an agricultural state. This means that at one time, most of the state's money came from products raised on farms and plantations. Until the twentieth century, most of Alabama's money came from cotton. But since the boll weevil destroyed many cotton crops, other types of crops have been planted. For instance, in 2005 Alabama was the third-largest producer of peanuts and peanut products in the United States. More than half a million acres in Alabama are planted with soybeans. Other crops that are raised in large amounts include corn, sweet potatoes,

The boll weevil hurt Alabama's economy, but it also helped it. If the insects had not destroyed so much cotton, farmers might not have been encouraged to grow profitable crops like peanuts and soybeans. In honor of this insect, the Boll Weevil Monument was erected in the town of Enterprise.

A natural gas plant towers over a cotton field. Cotton and natural gas are two of Alabama's most important crops.

watermelons, beans, and peas. Farmers also produce a lot of peaches, pecans, blueberries, and tomatoes.

Not all Alabama crops are used as food or in manufacturing. The state also provides plants that go toward the nursery industry. Garden shops throughout the state and around the country sell plants and flowers that have been grown in Alabama. These include azalea bushes, many types of flowers, small trees, and ground cover like ivy.

Crops are not the only way farmers make money. More money in agriculture is made in livestock. In 2003, Alabama

Alabama's grasses and warm weather are ideal for grazing livestock.

Recipe for Alabama Pecan Logs

Pecans are a popular product in the South. Follow this recipe to make a tasty pecan treat.

Ingredients:

1/2 pound sweet butter
1/2 cup powdered sugar
2 cups chopped pecans
1/2 teaspoon salt
1 cup flour
1 teaspoon vanilla

Have an adult preheat the oven to 325 degrees Fahrenheit. Grease a large cookie sheet with vegetable oil or shortening.

Ask an adult help you mix the butter until it is smooth. Slowly add the sugar, salt, flour, and vanilla.

When those ingredients are well-mixed, stir in the pecans.

Take a heaping spoonful of the batter and put it on a plate. Roll it into the shape of a log and place it on the cookie sheet. When the sheet is full, place it in the oven.

Bake the logs for 15 to 20 minutes. During this time, keep checking on them to make sure they do not burn.

When they are done, let them cool. Enjoy your nutty treat!

farmers owned more than one million cows. Some of these cows are used on dairy farms, but most are used for food. When the cattle are old enough and big enough, they are shipped to centers in Alabama or neighboring states. But the biggest farm product, according to the U.S. Department of Agriculture, is broiler chickens. These small chickens are grown and sold as food and make up almost 59 percent of the state's farm income.

A new type of farming in Alabama involves fish. In 2005, Alabama had about 25,000 water acres of fish farms. These farmers watch over the fish, making sure they eat a good diet and do not get sick. When the fish are big enough, they are sold to places like restaurants and grocery stores. In Alabama, a lot of catfish are raised in fish farms. Alabama was rated second in catfish production in 2005, and this industry is growing quickly. Some fish farmers also raise ornamental fish. These fish include koi—a large type of carp—and goldfish. People sometimes build ponds in their yards and stock them with koi. Smaller goldfish are usually kept in aquariums in people's homes.

Catfish farms are a growing part of the state's agricultural industry.

Most of Alabama's fish, however, are still caught in open waters such as the Gulf of Mexico or in Alabama's rivers and reservoirs. There are river-caught catfish, which is one of the most popular fish in Alabama, but there are also saltwater fish such as groupers and snappers that are caught in the Gulf.

Alabama's shrimp and shellfish industry used to provide millions of dollars to the state's economy. Unfortunately, this industry was hit hard by Hurricane Katrina. But Alabamians are working hard to make this industry profitable once again.

Mining

Alabama has large deposits of coal and limestone. These are used to make iron and steel, two important products for Alabama's economy. Alabama is the only state that has all the ingredients located within the state to make iron and steel. Alabama is the largest supplier of cast-iron and steel pipe products.

The business of drilling for resources such as oil and natural gas has been expanding in the state over the past twenty years. Today, Alabama ranks ninth in the country as a major producer of natural gas. Natural gas is used to create energy and heat for homes and businesses.

An worker checks on an oil pump.

This tugboat is pushing a barge of wood chips along the Tombigbee River.

Manufacturing

More than 290,000 Alabamians worked in the state's manufacturing industry. Items that are made in Alabama include everything from food and tobacco products to leather, paper, and wood products. Chemicals, automobiles, plastics, computers, jewelry, toys, and furniture are also manufactured in Alabama.

Many companies from other parts of the worlds, such as Japan and Korea have built car factories in Alabama in recent years. Other large companies in the state manufacture important government-related products such as aerospace equipment and missiles.

There are also large companies in Alabama that process food. This includes human food such as candy and ice cream, but also pet food. Other companies use Alabama's cotton crops to make textiles, or materials for things such as curtains, towels, and clothes.

Alabama's lumber industry is profitable. A large amount of wood is shipped to other parts of the country. But Alabama factories also process the wood, turning into useful products like wood chips, furniture, or paper.

The Service Industry

Of all the different categories of jobs in Alabama, the service industry employs the most people in the state. The service industry includes people who provide a service to the people. For example, people who work at grocery stores, insurance companies, schools, hospitals, gas stations, hotels, amusement parks, movie theaters, shopping malls, police and fire departments are all a part of the service industry.

Tourism is a huge part of Alabama's service industry. Alabama's natural beauty attracts tourists from the other states and people from all over the world. Its historic sites and busy cities also bring in visitors. Visitors who come to Alabama stay in hotels, eat in restaurants, buy gas, and spend on entertainment and souvenirs. All of this money helps the state's economy and jobs are created and maintained to support the tourism industry. In 2005, the tourism industry contributed more than $7 billion to Alabama's economy.

Visitors to Alabama can learn about the state's history at sites like Consitution Hall Village in Huntsville.

Products & Resources

Catfish

Catfish farming has become one of Alabama's fastest-growing agricultural activities in recent years. There are many different kinds of catfish, but the channel catfish is the most common type raised on the fish farms. Although they can grow to almost 50 pounds, most channel catfish weigh between 10 and 20 pounds.

Steel

Alabama's first steel mill opened in 1880, and ten years later, steel was Alabama's biggest industry. Today, steel continues to be an important product in Alabama. Many products are made of steel but some of the most decorative steel products from Alabama are wrought iron furniture pieces. The wrought iron is twisted and curled to make interesting designs.

Eggs

The average American eats more than two hundred eggs each year. That is about as many eggs as one healthy chicken can produce in a year. Alabama has a lot of chickens and a lot of eggs. On large farms, chickens are housed in big buildings. The eggs from these chickens are collected by machines. The eggs are sorted by size and packaged into cartons. Alabama eggs are then shipped out to grocery stores throughout the state and around the country.

Wood Products

Two-thirds of Alabama is still covered in forests, giving the state the second-most extensive forest cover in the United States. Some of the trees that are grown in Alabama's forests are made into paper products. The trees are sent to a mill, where they are trimmed, chopped, and boiled into a pulp. Then the pulp is laid out on large screens and dried. Later the dried pulp is pressed to form paper.

Aerospace and Flight Research

Researchers at the George C. Marshall Space Flight Center in Huntsville produced the rocket that propelled the first landing on the moon. But that is not all they have done over the years. They have also produced the tools that maintain the Hubble Space Telescope, and their designs were used to create the International Space Station. The Marshall Space Flight Center provides many jobs for Alabamians.

Fishing

Sport fishing is part of the state's tourism industry. Alabamians, as well as people from other places, enjoy fishing in Alabama's rivers, lakes, and streams. Many also take big boats out into the Gulf and spend the day catching big tuna or swordfish. More than 800,000 Alabamian's applied for fishing licenses in 2005.

"One of the greatest things Alabama did for the state economy," says Dick Ptomey of Autaugaville, "is build those golf courses." What Ptomey is referring to also has the whole nation talking. The state invested some of its money in a system of eight golf courses, located all over Alabama. These new golf courses have been ranked as some of the best in the United States. Because of this, Alabamians not only have a chance to have enjoy golfing, but people from all over the world are now traveling to Alabama to try out these new courses. These golfing visitors bring in a great deal of money to the state's tourism industry.

The Future

Between 2000 and 2006, Alabama has seen positive growth in many different areas. Money coming in from taxes has increased, which in turn helps the state run smoothly. And by September 2006, the state had added more than 26,000 more jobs. Experts say that this rapid economic growth might not continue at such a fast rate. But they think that Alabama's economy will still continue to improve and grow. This is good news for Alabamians. The future is bright for Alabamians as they continue to work hard and make a living in the Heart of Dixie.

In 1895 Alabama selected an official state flag. The flag displays a red diagonal cross on a white background. The flag was designed after the Confederate battle flag used during the Civil War.

Alabama's state seal shows a rough map of Alabama, its rivers, and the territories around Alabama. (These territories would later become states.) This seal was originally used as the territorial seal in the 1800s. It was made the official state seal in 1819, but was replaced by a different seal in the late 1860s. In 1939 Alabama's state government decided to use the original seal, and it has been the official seal ever since.

State Flag and Seal

ALABAMA

Pickwick Lake

Florence

72

Birthplace of Helen Keller

43

157

Wheeler Lake

Decatur

Tennessee River

U.S. Space and Rocket Center and Space Camp

65

Huntsville

Russell Cave National Monument

Sequoyah Caverns

75

Little River Canyon National Preserve

Dismals Canyon

24

William B. Bankhead National Forest

78

Natural Bridge

5

Lewis Smith Lake

Wheeler National Wildlife Refuge

Cathedral Caverns State Park

431

278

59

Weiss Lake

Gadsden

H. Neely Henn Lake

278

17

Rickwood Caverns State Park

Sipsey River

Talladega Superspeedway

Anniston

20

Cheaha Mountain

R.L. Harris Reservoir

West Point Lake

431

82

Birmingham

Bankhead Lake

459

Logan Martin Lake

De Soto Caverns Park

77

9

Tallapoosa River

Tuscaloosa

20 59

Lake Tuscaloosa

Black Warrior River

Lay Lake

Coosa River

Talladega National Forest

65

Mitchell Lake

21

Horseshoe Bend National Military Park

Lake Martin

Auburn

85

280

Demopolis

80

First White House of the Confederacy

Selma

Fort Toulouse/ Jackson State Historic Park

Montgomery

Tuskegee

82

Old Cahawba Site of First State Capital

28

William "Bill" Dannelly Reservoir

Eufaula

Walter F. George Reservoir

Tombigbee River

10

Alabama River

231

331

51

10

95

Chattahoochee River

84

Jackson

Poarch Creek Indian Reservation

65

55

Gantt Lake

Point "A" Lake

41

29

Conecuh National Forest

59

Opp

Conecuh River

Pea River

Lake Tholocco

Enterprise

Dothan

45

217

Big Creek Lake

Mobile River

Tensaw River

112

10

Atmore

Mobile

Foley

Mobile Bay

Bon Secour Bay

Perdido Bay

Mississippi Sound

INTRACOASTAL WATERWAY

GULF OF MEXICO

N
W   E
S

miles
0   40

		Interstate Highway		City or Town		Highest Point in the State
		U.S. Highway		Indian Reservation		National Preserve
		State Highway		National Monument		Historic Site
		State Capital		Wildlife Refuge		National Forest

Alabama

Words by Julia Strudwick Tutwiler
Music by Edna Gockel Gussen

1. Al - a-bam - a, Al - a - bam - a, We will aye be true to thee,

From thy South-ern shores where grow - eth By the _ sea thy or - ange tree.

To _ thy North - ern vale where flow - eth Deep and blue _ thy Ten - nes - see,

Al - a-bam - a, Al - a - bam - a, We will _ aye be true to thee!

State Song

More About Alabama

Books

Martin, Michael A. *Alabama: The Heart of Dixie*. Milwaukee, WI: World Almanac Library, 2002.

Nobleman, Marc Tyler. *Rosa Parks*. Milwaukee, WI: World Almanac Library, 2002.

Wilson, Martin. *Uniquely Alabama*. Chicago: Heinemann Library, 2004.

Web Sites

Alabama Department of Archives and History Kids' Page
http://www.archives.state.al.us/kidspage/kids.html

Alabama Department of Tourism and Travel
http://www.touralabama.org

Alabama Kids' Page
http://www.alabama.gov/portal/interact/kidspage.jsp

Official State of Alabama Homepage
http://www.alabama.gov

About the Author

Joyce Hart, who was raised in the South, has worked as an educator, an assistant librarian, an editor, and a desktop publisher. She is currently a freelance writer and the author of several books. Her brother-in-law, Dick Ptomey, grew up in Alabama, can trace his Alabama ancestry back several generations, and had a lot of fun telling Ms. Hart stories about Alabama as she wrote this book.

Index

Page numbers in **boldface** are illustrations.